EXPLORING ART

ANIME AND MANGA

by Christine Ha

BrightPoint Press

San Diego, CA

BrightPoint Press

an imprint of ReferencePoint Press, Inc.
Printed in the United States

For more information, contact:
BrightPoint Press
PO Box 27779
San Diego, CA 92198
www.BrightPointPress.com

LIBRARY OF CONGRESS CATALOGING-IN-PUBLICATION DATA

Names: Ha, Christine, 1997- author.
Title: Anime and manga / by Christine Ha.
Description: San Diego, CA : BrightPoint Press, [2022] | Series: Exploring art | Includes bibliographical references and index. | Audience: Grades 7-9
Identifiers: LCCN 2021009684 (print) | LCCN 2021009685 (eBook) | ISBN 9781678201166 (hardcover) | ISBN 9781678201173 (eBook)
Subjects: LCSH: Animated films--Japan--Juvenile literature. | Comic books, strips, etc.--Japan--Juvenile literature.
Classification: LCC NC1766.J3 H3 2022 (print) | LCC NC1766.J3 (eBook) | DDC 791.43/340952--dc23
LC record available at https://lccn.loc.gov/2021009684
LC eBook record available at https://lccn.loc.gov/2021009685

CONTENTS

AT A GLANCE

- Anime and manga are art forms from Japan. They are known for their distinct style and immersive storytelling. Manga are comic books, and anime are animated cartoons.
- The word *anime* comes from the English word "animation." In Japan, *anime* describes all animation. But the rest of the world usually uses the word *anime* to describe animation that comes from Japan.
- The word *manga* comes from an artist named Katsushika Hokusai. He was a well-known artist who compiled his works into a book titled *Hokusai Manga*.
- The first manga were published in magazines in Japan after World War II (1939–1945). Manga magazines are still popular today.

- Anime became popular in Japan in the 1960s. Changes in the following decades improved the look of anime and broadened its appeal.
- Creating anime and manga is complicated. There are many steps.
- The anime and manga industries can be challenging and competitive for artists.
- Now, anime and manga are worldwide sensations. Fans around the world celebrate the art forms in many fun ways.

THE MANY WORLDS OF ANIME AND MANGA

When Adrian was growing up, anime played on TV every Saturday morning. There were many different anime shows, but Adrian's favorite was *Pokémon*. He never missed an episode. Adrian loved how the series let him experience a totally new world. He also enjoyed the unique

***Pokémon* has been a popular anime and video game series for decades.**

art style. The colorful drawings transported him into the story.

Adrian's love for anime only grew as he got older. Some people felt animated shows were only for kids. But Adrian soon realized there was truly an anime for everyone.

Anime characters played sports and joined bands. They explored futuristic worlds with giant robots and spacecraft. They fought with magic and saved the world. And the animation only got better and better over time. The backgrounds could be incredibly detailed. The action scenes were intense. Adrian could not wait to see even more exciting anime come out.

JAPANESE ART, WORLDWIDE APPEAL

Anime and manga are art forms from Japan. They are known for their unique

Many anime films are shown in movie theaters in Japan.

style. Throughout their development, these art forms have varied greatly. But anime and manga have often included attention to detail in both characters and scenery. In addition, the characters often have large eyes and expressive features.

Manga are comics and graphic novels. In Japanese, *manga* means "whimsical pictures." The word *whimsical* means imaginative and unpredictable. The origins of manga can be traced back hundreds of years.

In Japan, the word *anime* refers to all types of animation. People in other countries use *anime* to describe Japanese animation specifically. Although animation in Japan can be traced back to 1917, anime as it is known today was created in the 1960s. In the late 1980s and 1990s, anime spread worldwide. Today, people around the globe love and celebrate anime and manga.

Big crowds flock to anime events around the world.

CHAPTER ONE

WHAT ARE ANIME AND MANGA?

Anime and manga use pictures to tell stories. These stories can be from many **genres** and for different age groups. Some are funny and heartwarming. Others are serious and dark. Some are for kids. Others are for teenagers or adults. Anime and manga feature diverse

Stores in Japan offer anime and manga for all audiences.

worlds, characters, and situations. Many anime and manga include relatable and realistic characters.

Master animator Hayao Miyazaki once said animated films let viewers explore other lives they could have lived. He said these other lives were like "lost possibilities."

Miyazaki explained, "For example, I might have been the captain of a pirate ship, sailing with a lovely princess by my side. . . . There are selves which are lost possibilities, and selves that could have been. . . . And I think that's exactly why the fantasy worlds of cartoon movies so strongly represent our hopes and yearnings. They illustrate a world of lost possibilities for us."[1]

Modern anime and manga have a distinct visual style. This style helps them tell stories. The most defining feature of anime and manga is their characters' eyes. The eyes are often large and exaggerated. In Japan, eyes are seen as strong emotional indicators. They can tell viewers a character's true emotions, even if the character's words or actions say otherwise. Eyes may also indicate a character's personality. Larger eyes usually show a person is **earnest** and sweet.

DOUJINSHI

A unique form of manga is called doujinshi. This means "one-person magazine." These are self-published works that appeal to a specific audience. They are typically fan creations that use characters from existing media. However, they can also be original stories. Doujinshi are often distributed online or sold at conventions. Some physical stores carry doujinshi as well.

More serious characters or villains typically have narrower eyes.

Expressions and actions are often exaggerated too. If a character is crying, tears may flow like rivers out of his eyes. If the character is embarrassed, his whole face might turn red. Steam might even rise from his head.

Despite this exaggeration, other parts of anime and manga often have a dedication to realism. Artists work to ensure quality even with challenging production schedules. They keep the art consistent. Each frame has a purpose and adds to the story.

Anime-style backgrounds are often realistic and rich with detail.

Backgrounds and objects such as food are given special care. Most backgrounds in anime and manga are grounded in reality. When possible, they look like the real places they are based on.

Makoto Shinkai is a director known for his attention to detail. He spoke about this in regard to his 2019 film *Weathering with You*. He said, "I want people to feel as if this is something taking place in our world right now. It's not a piece of fiction that has nothing to do with you and I—it's happening here and now."[2] Detailed objects and beautiful backgrounds help with storytelling. They make the stories more immersive.

WHAT MAKES MANGA UNIQUE?

Manga is a style of comic art. Each page is made of one or more **panels**. These panels are called *koma* in Japanese. Panels

A fan in Russia reads a manga magazine.

contain drawings of the characters and backgrounds. Unlike English, Japanese is written vertically and read from right to left. That means manga is read top to bottom, right to left. Each page's flow starts at the panel in the top right corner and ends at the panel on the bottom left. This is different from how comics written in English are read.

Panels may also contain speech bubbles. These indicate that a character is talking or thinking. Different types of bubbles express a character's emotions. Visual sound effects are also common in manga. These are called *kakimoji*. Sound effect text is often stylized to fit the scenario. These sound effects use **onomatopoeia**. For example, the Japanese sound effect *ban* indicates a loud banging sound, such as slamming a door. Sometimes sound effects can even

PARTS OF A MANGA PAGE

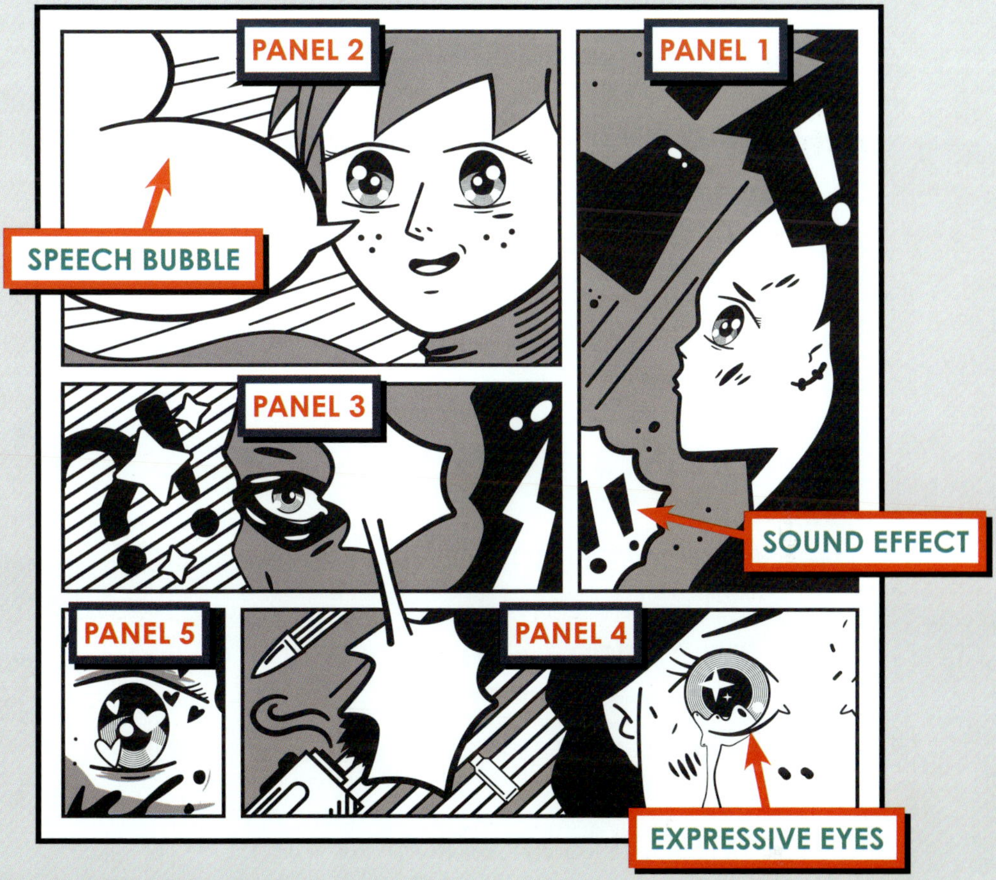

Manga are read top to bottom, right to left. They have many different features to help tell stories.

be used to convey a character's mood. For example, the Japanese phrase *piku piku* is used to express frustration. The sound is supposed to emulate the twitching of an eyebrow, especially when someone is at the end of his patience. The use of written sound effects helps shape a story's feeling.

WHAT MAKES ANIME UNIQUE?

The word *anime* comes from the English word "animation." Sometimes anime is based on manga or other existing media. Other times, it tells original stories.

Anime comes in many forms. Usually, anime series air weekly on TV. They are made up of episodes that run thirty to sixty minutes each. Anime may also be full-length films. These tend to be higher quality and

Fans tune in to watch new episodes of their favorite anime series on TV each week.

have a bigger budget. Sometimes, anime are original video animations (OVAs). These may be extra stories connected to a series. They may also be original stories. OVAs allow studios and artists to experiment with styles and formats. These are often released on home video.

Anime shares many characteristics with manga. However, anime adds color, animation, and audio. Anime is known for its artistry. The characters are vibrant, lively, and fun to watch. The backgrounds are beautiful. Animations are fluid. Each scene works to convey particular emotions. Great voice acting and music can make anime an engaging experience. These factors have made many anime series and movies memorable and influential.

Colin Decker runs a company called Funimation. This company **translates** and distributes many anime series outside of

Voice actors from around the world help adapt anime series for local audiences.

Japan. Decker explained why global fans connect with anime. He said, “A lot of what is appealing about anime for audiences around the world is that it represents such a different [point of view].”[3]

TYPES OF ANIME AND MANGA

Different kinds of anime and manga are for different audiences. There are five main categories. They are sorted by age and gender. Those divisions can be further divided into smaller subgenres.

The first category is *kodomomuke*. This translates to "targeted toward children." These stories tend to be simple and colorful. Like Western cartoons, these often teach children morals and values. Some examples are *Doraemon* and *Hello Kitty*.

Next, there is *shōnen*. *Shōnen* translates to "young boy." These are targeted toward

Hello Kitty has become one of the most famous anime characters internationally.

teen boys. Shōnen stories focus on action and adventure. *Dragon Ball Z*, *Naruto*, *Bleach*, and *One Piece* are examples of this genre.

Shōjo means "young girl." It is the female equivalent to shōnen. Shōjo may feature action and adventure. But there is a greater focus on relationships and friendships. Some examples include *Sailor Moon*, *Ouran High School Host Club*, and *Fruits Basket.*

Next, there is *seinen*. Seinen is targeted toward older males, usually those in their late teens or early twenties. These works tend to have darker, more violent narratives. While seinen may have comedy, they tend to be more mature. *Ghost in the Shell*, *Akira*, and *Berserk* are some notable examples of seinen series.

Goku from Dragon Ball Z *(left)* and Doraemon *(right)* are popular anime characters from two different genres.

Lastly, *josei* is aimed at adult women. Unlike shōjo's idealized romances, josei stories focus on more realistic friendships and relationships. This genre includes works like *NANA* and *Paradise Kiss*.

Works are often marketed as certain genres. But that does not mean that other people outside of the **demographic** cannot enjoy the stories. It simply comes down to personal tastes and interests. There are many examples of works that cross these

ANIME HAIR

Anime characters often have crazy and colorful hair. For example, it's almost impossible to read shōnen without encountering characters with spiky, gravity-defying hair. Hair in anime is often used to indicate personality. Blue-haired characters are often cool, calm, and collected. Red-haired characters may be fiery and angry. Girls with pigtails are usually youthful and feminine. Those with low ponytails are often motherly and kind.

***A fan in Italy dresses up as a character from the hit manga and anime* Full Metal Alchemist.**

divisions. For example, *Full Metal Alchemist* is categorized as shōnen. But it became a popular series among all ages and genders.

CHAPTER TWO

WHAT IS THE HISTORY OF ANIME AND MANGA?

Modern manga was not created until after World War II (1939–1945). But its origins date back to the 1100s and 1200s CE. One work from this time was called *Choju-Giga*. This means "Scrolls of Frolicking Animals." In these scrolls, artists

One of Hokusai's most famous works shows a huge ocean wave near Mount Fuji.

would draw animals' legs in a way that made them look like they were running. Drawing things to imitate motion can still be seen in modern manga. Artist Katsushika Hokusai was among the first to use the word *manga*. In 1814, he made a book of his works named *Hokusai Manga*.

MODERN MANGA BEGINS

After World War II, American soldiers occupied Japan. During this time, Japan was exposed to Western culture. This included American comics. These works inspired modern manga. Manga artists, or *mangaka*, made their own comics.

Soon, magazines and newspapers were publishing manga stories. Manga magazines had a huge impact on the growth of the art form. Manga critic Haruyuki Nakano says, "Comic magazines are the first place where manga artists were given a chance to show their work. Without them, manga artists would not have been born."[4] These publications usually featured multiple series. Each issue included a chapter of each series. Manga magazines became popular in the 1960s.

The publisher Shueisha became a big player in this industry. Shueisha released several magazines. Many of them still exist today. The publisher's top

GOD OF MANGA

One of the most famous manga published in early manga magazines was *Astro Boy*. The manga was written by Osamu Tezuka. He is often called the God of Manga. He is credited for introducing the distinctive large eyes used in manga and anime.

magazine was *Shōnen Jump.* Others included *Weekly Shōnen Magazine* and *Weekly Shōnen Sunday*. They featured well-established manga artists. *Shōnen Jump* often published manga by new artists. These stories took risks and

SHŌNEN JUMP

***Shōnen Jump* is the best-selling manga magazine. Since 1968, it has sold more than 7.5 billion copies. In 2003, a US version launched. The US *Shonen Jump* shifted online in 2012. In Japan, most bookstores and convenience stories stock *Shōnen Jump*. However, the US magazine was not available as widely. The publisher decided digital publishing would bring the magazine to more people.**

pushed social boundaries. As a result, they captured a wide audience.

EARLY ANIME

Animation in Japan can be traced back to the early 1900s. Most animation made at that time was government **propaganda**. It was in black and white. Animations were made up of just a few frames. Characters would do simple actions. The backgrounds were often static.

It wasn't until the 1960s that anime aired on TV. Osamu Tezuka's *Astro Boy* was a pioneering series. It was adapted from Tezuka's manga of the same name.

A statue of the legendary Astro Boy character in Japan

Astro Boy established many standards and styles. At the time, animation studios had small staffs and tight budgets. This led to a technique called "limited animation." Moveable joints like elbows and knees were drawn simply. Backgrounds were plain. Features such as hair and accessories had more detail. This made characters look distinctive. At the same time, they were easy to animate. Traditional animation might use tens of thousands of frames. A limited animation show like *Astro Boy* needed only about 1,500 drawings per episode.

As the 1960s continued, more people in Japan got color televisions. This sparked new changes in anime. Color led to more expressive backgrounds. Older shows used simple shading. Now artists could create beautiful landscapes. Character details also improved. Animation became more fluid. New series attracted older audiences.

ANIME FROM THE 1970s TO TODAY

The 1970s and 1980s brought more changes. Many anime began focusing more on details, especially facial expressions. Several studios worked on creating dynamic backgrounds. Many studios also experimented with styles. Consistency in quality and **continuity** improved too. These qualities helped anime build even more immersive worlds.

Today, Studio Ghibli is one of the most well-known studios. The studio revolutionized anime. It had realistic character animation and detail. Its

The Gundam anime franchise, which began in 1979 and features giant fighting robots, became a pop culture phenomenon. A life-size Gundam statue was even built in Japan.

background art was especially impressive. Studio Ghibli's success led to a boom in anime.

The 1988 science-fiction anime film *Akira* was important and influential. Its attention to detail in its animation and cityscapes was stunning. *Akira* showed a rich and mature sci-fi world. Viewers saw that cartoons could address mature topics and issues in society. Christopher Bolton is a professor who studies anime. He described the impact of *Akira*. Bolton said, “I think it announced to the American public a kind of potential for this medium, which generated a lot of excitement and has played out in the last 30 years as this kind of anime boom.”[5]

Works in the 1990s focused heavily on realism. Anime creators used muted color palettes, accurate proportions, and smooth animation. New technology

A billboard advertises a new release of Akira on home video in Japan.

brought changes to anime. Creators could now draw and animate digitally. Digital art has many advantages. It allows artists to be creative in new ways. Digital drawing programs let them create cleaner, crisper, and more-realistic art than ever before.

CHAPTER THREE

HOW ARE ANIME AND MANGA MADE TODAY?

Creating a manga usually involves teamwork. An editor, a mangaka, and often a team of assistants work together. Making manga is challenging. Artists have to complete a chapter every week. This continues until their story ends or the magazine stops publishing it.

Digital drawing tablets have given manga artists a new way to work.

Drawing manga has many steps. These steps were once done all on paper. Today, many artists use computer programs.

First, the editor and mangaka create a story. The artist then sketches out rough drawings and dialogue. This is called the *ne-mu*. This is the most time-consuming step. There are often four to five rounds of revisions.

An editor approves the ne-mu. Then, the artist continues to develop the plot and characters. He may even conduct interviews for research. Throughout this process, the editor provides advice.

The next step is called the *genko*. In this step, the mangaka inks his drawings. On the genko, the mangaka shows where he wants assistants to fill in black. He may also indicate what textures or screentones to place. Sometimes assistants help by drawing the backgrounds. Assistants do a variety of tasks to help a mangaka. After the genko is done, that week's manga is complete. The mangaka and his team start drafting the next ne-mu, and the cycle begins again.

SCREENTONES

Screentones are adhesive sheets with patterns printed on them. Originally, manga magazines were printed only in black and white. Patterns such as dots and lines were added for visual interest. The sheets would be cut to the appropriate sizes and shapes and then pasted onto a panel. Today many artists have shifted to digital programs that can recreate screentone textures.

In the meantime, the editor does other tasks. She visits bookstores to gather readers' opinions. The editor also organizes reader events, offers autographed gifts, and works on marketing. The editor stays involved throughout the entire process.

MANGA ASSISTANTS

Some artists hire up to ten assistants, depending on how complicated the production is. Assistants refer to the mangaka as *sensei*, which means teacher. This is a common title of respect in Japan. Doctors and lawyers may also be called *sensei* as a way to show respect.

DISTRIBUTING MANGA

Manga are typically printed in black and white. Only special releases are in color. Manga are typically found in magazines. *Shōnen Jump*, *Ciao*, and *CoroCoro Comic* are a few examples. Usually these magazines host several different manga. They print one chapter from each manga weekly or monthly. These stories are later collected into volumes.

It can be tough for manga to keep going. For example, *Shōnen Jump* has a survey in every magazine that asks for readers' opinions. The higher a series

Manga magazines are widely available in Japanese stores.

ranks, the closer to the front it is printed in the next issue. Unpopular series are discontinued. Therefore, artists strive to be better than their competition. Manga artist Kumagai Kyoko says, "There's an urge to be better than the next person, to come up with a big hit. This sense of competition spurs people on and helps refine their skills."[6] This industry mindset results in high-quality manga.

Luckily, magazines are not the only way to get published. A new mangaka can apply for a manga award or enter a contest. These contests usually have a theme that the artist must use. Artists can submit their work for a chance to be published.

The internet has been a great resource for aspiring mangaka. Manga magazines have shifted online. There are also websites

Today's fans can catch up on their favorite manga on tablets and smartphones.

where artists can self-publish their works. Social media has made it easy for artists to share their work.

DEVELOPING ANIME

Anime once used traditional drawings, but in recent years anime production has become more and more digital. Computer graphics have also been introduced into anime. These advances can help make production easier and simpler.

As with manga, anime begins with an idea. Sometimes anime are based on manga or other existing works, like novels or video games. Other times, they are original stories. In preproduction, the writer creates a script. The director then reviews and approves it.

Next comes the **storyboard**, or *ekonte*. This includes drawings, actions, and the length of each shot. The storyboard helps plan the flow of the anime. In Western animation, the storyboard is typically completed by a group of animators. In Japan, it is often done by a single director. It should be detailed enough to make the story clear, but rough enough to give the animators room for creativity.

The next step is layout. This step is also called *daiichi genga*, or first key animation. It includes rough drawings of the characters, effects, and backgrounds. It usually includes instructions for background staff. A time sheet is also created at this time. This breaks down how the shot should look and

Artists storyboard their anime scenes before beginning the animation process.

makes it easier for anyone else who works on it later on in the process.

BRINGING ANIME TO LIFE

The animation work is completed by two types of animators. The first are called key animators. They draw the important frames in each scene. The first frame, the middle frame, and the last frame are considered the most important. They are known as key frames. Key animators look at reference drawings to make sure all the details are correct. The second type of animators are in-betweener animators. They create the drawings between the key images. They make sure the animation flows smoothly. A thirty-minute episode may include a few thousand drawings.

Next, the drawings are reviewed by in-between supervisors. They look for mistakes and make sure the animation

An exhibit on Studio Ghibli shows drawings from the making of the famous studio's anime films.

looks like it is supposed to. Then, the episode director reviews the work. The episode director is in charge of the episode. He or she works under a series director who oversees the overall project.

The animation director's check is next. There are usually one or two animation directors per episode. There can be up to ten depending on the production. They work under a general animation director. Animation directors review the quality and accuracy of the drawings and animations. They may also draw in corrections.

After the layout is approved, work on scenery and backgrounds begins separately. First, they are drafted on paper and reviewed. Then, they go to the landscape department. In the past, backgrounds were completely hand

Giant robots, called mecha, are popular in anime. Digital techniques can make these complex machines easier to animate.

painted. Now, there has been a shift to digital painting. Painting by hand is still done sometimes, but usually digital painting is more efficient.

The next step is second key animation, or *daini genga*. This is where the first key animation is retraced and cleaned up. Then, it undergoes another checking process.

This is followed by compositing. The backgrounds and animation are added together. People work on coloring and shading. A set color palette ensures coloring stays consistent.

After compositing comes the effects. Here, the team takes the fully colored animations and adds effects. This includes glowing lights, glints on swords, blurs for fast motion, and other things.

Finally, the last step is postproduction. Editors make sure a finished episode fits within the thirty-minute broadcast time. The audio team adds voices, sound effects, and music. The anime is now complete.

PROBLEMS WITH ANIME PRODUCTION

Like the manga industry, the anime industry is very competitive. The industry works to keep budgets and costs low. Most animators are overworked and underpaid. Jun Sugawara is an animator. He is aware of this problem. He says, "It takes genius to create beautiful hand-drawn animation, and animators' skills are not valued." Sugawara runs an organization working to improve conditions in the anime industry.

Quoted in Eric Margolis, "The Dark Side of Japan's Anime Industry," Vox, *July 2, 2019. www.vox.com.*

CHAPTER FOUR

WHAT IS THE CULTURAL IMPACT OF ANIME AND MANGA?

Anime and manga are popular worldwide. Manga are sold at many bookstores. Anime shows are on TV. Anime films are shown in theatres. Fans can also stream anime online. They can read manga on computers and tablets.

Viewers in Japan and across the globe enjoy anime series on TV.

Many manga and anime have even been turned into live-action productions. This happened with 2017's *Death Note* and 2019's *Alita: Battle Angel*. Western streaming services have brought anime from Japan. They have even produced original shows. Today, anime and manga have far-reaching effects. They have influenced many parts of our culture.

GROWING POPULARITY

The 1990s were a huge decade for anime and manga. Many works established the potential of the art form. Hits like *Sailor Moon*, *Pokémon*, and *Dragon Ball Z* were shown on American TV. They helped turn a generation of kids into anime fans. Works like *Neon Genesis Evangelion* and *Cowboy Bebop* attracted older viewers. They showed that animation was not just for

***An exhibit in Japan showcases the history of* Sailor Moon.**

children. They featured mature themes and stunning visuals.

Anime and manga remained popular in the 2000s. The internet helped promote global interest. Fans around the world could discuss their favorite works. Many well-known series appeared in this era. They include *One Piece*, *Naruto*, and *Bleach*. Series were made into movies, video games, and merchandise. This made them even more popular. American audiences had more access to anime and manga than ever.

The action-adventure series *Full Metal Alchemist* became popular in this era. So did darker, more mature works like *Samurai Champloo* and *Death Note.* Studio Ghibli had a continued influence. It helped popularize anime internationally. In 2002, its film *Spirited Away* won the Oscar for Best Animated Feature. It became a classic.

The series One Piece is so popular that there is an entire store dedicated to it in Japan.

Some Western animated shows even started to look like anime. These included series such as *Teen Titans*, *Avatar: The Last Airbender*, and *Samurai Jack*. In this era, global fans also began to see their favorite anime series sooner. In the past, they had to wait until after the Japanese releases. Online services began showing subtitled episodes the same day they aired in Japan. By 2017, countries outside Japan provided the anime industry with nearly half of its revenue. Countries such as South Korea, China, and Taiwan became major

CONVENTIONS & COSPLAY

The boom of anime culture led to American anime conventions. These are large gatherings that allow fans to celebrate their shared passion. They often take place over several days. They include panels where fans can meet voice actors. There are also opportunities to purchase merchandise. Visitors also commonly cosplay. The term *cosplay* comes from the words "costume play." Cosplay is when fans dress up as characters they like.

markets. The 2010s also saw more anime being produced. Technology helped lower production costs. Audiences saw many new series in this period.

THE POWER OF TECHNOLOGY

A series called *One-Punch Man* shows how technology has changed things. It began as an independent online manga in 2009. The creator was a manga fan. He went by the name ONE. The drawing style was crude. Still, people flocked to the story. It was about a superhero so powerful he could beat any foe with just one punch. As a result, he gets bored and searches for an

Many fans love to dress up as their favorite characters from anime and manga.

enemy who can challenge him. The story lines have a mix of humor and action.

In 2012, an experienced manga creator teamed up with ONE. They remade *One-Punch Man* for *Weekly Shōnen Jump*.

The art was much improved. The series gained more popularity. Within a few years, a major studio made it into an anime. Thanks to the power of the internet, *One-Punch Man* went from a webcomic to a globally popular anime.

ANIME IN WESTERN MUSIC VIDEOS

Anime has entered mainstream American culture. That includes the world of music. In 2020, R&B artist The Weeknd released a music video for his song "Snowchild." It was in an anime style. The video was produced by the first Black-owned anime studio, D'ART Shtajio. Another well-known example is "Shelter" by Porter Robinson and Madeon. The video was produced by anime production company A-1 Pictures.

Anime movies also experienced a rise in popularity. In the past, only a few anime movies came to US theaters. However, in the 2010s, these movies appeared more regularly. The success of 2016's *A Silent Voice* led to a campaign to nominate it for an Oscar. In 2016, Makoto Shinkai's film *Your Name* set box office records in Japan. Shinkai's next film, 2019's *Weathering with You*, was another big success.

A GLOBALLY POPULAR ART FORM

Doryun Chong helps run an art museum in Hong Kong. He says, "Anime possesses an incredible narrative imagination." Chong

Manga can now be found in most major US bookstores.

says this has led to its "global success."[7] Manga has become big in the West, too. Kristen McLean studies the book industry. She says, "Manga is one area of the US book market that is catching fire." McLean explains that manga appeals to "a whole new set of younger and more diverse book buyers."[8] In today's world, anime and manga are bigger now than ever before.

GLOSSARY

continuity
consistency between different parts of an anime or manga

conventions
events where fans come together to celebrate their favorite books, shows, or movies

demographic
an audience for a particular kind of media

earnest
sincere and honest

genres
categories of media

onomatopoeia
a word that sounds like the noise it describes, such as "boom" or "meow"

panels
the outlines around individual images that make up a manga

propaganda
information that is created and spread to influence an audience to think a certain way

storyboard
a set of drawings used to plan out an anime

translates
changes the written or spoken parts of media from one language to another

SOURCE NOTES

CHAPTER ONE: WHAT ARE ANIME AND MANGA?

1. Quoted in Beckett Mufson, "18 Genius Hayao Miyazaki Quotes to Celebrate His 76th Birthday," *Vice*, January 5, 2017. www.vice.com.

2. Quoted in Matt Schley, "Makoto Shinkai Weathers the Storm," *Japan Times*, n.d. https://features.japantimes.co.jp.

3. Quoted in Cecilia D'Anastasio, "There's Something Super Weird About Netflix Anime," *Wired*, November 12, 2020. www.wired.com.

CHAPTER TWO: WHAT IS THE HISTORY OF ANIME AND MANGA?

4. Quoted in Minoru Matsutani, "Manga: Heart of Pop Culture," *Japan Times*, May 26, 2009. https://japantimes.co.jp.

5. Quoted in Hau Chu, "Why the Pioneering Japanese Anime 'Akira' Is Still Relevant 30 Years Later," *Washington Post*, July 13, 2018. www.washingtonpost.com.

CHAPTER THREE: HOW ARE ANIME AND MANGA MADE TODAY?

6. Quoted in "The Creation of Manga." *Trends in Japan*, 2017. https://web-japan.org.

CHAPTER FOUR: WHAT IS THE CULTURAL IMPACT OF ANIME AND MANGA?

7. Quoted in Emiko Jozuka, "Japanese Anime: From 'Disney of the East' to a Global Industry Worth Billions," *CNN*, July 28, 2019. www.cnn.com.

8. Quoted in "Sales of Manga Books Are on the Rise in the United States, the NPD Group Says," *NPD*, June 3, 2019. www.npd.com.

FOR FURTHER RESEARCH

BOOKS

Kerry Dinmont, *Animation*. San Diego, CA: BrightPoint Press, 2022.

Andrea C. Nakaya, *Growing Up in Japan*. San Diego, CA: ReferencePoint Press, 2018.

Tom Streissguth, *The Art of Anime and Manga*. San Diego, CA: ReferencePoint Press, 2020.

INTERNET SOURCES

Emiko Jozuka, "Japanese Anime: From 'Disney of the East' to a Global Industry Worth Billions," *CNN*, July 28, 2019. www.cnn.com.

Ryoko Matsuba and Alfred Haft, "Manga: A Brief History in 12 Works," *British Museum*, December 5, 2018. https://blog.britishmuseum.org.

Mark Trainer, "Anime's Supersized US Audience," *Share America*, June 28, 2017. https://share.america.gov.

WEBSITES

Anime Expo
www.anime-expo.org

Anime Expo is one of the oldest and largest anime conventions in the United States.

Japan National Tourism Organization
www.japan.travel/en

The website of the Japan National Tourism Organization includes information about visiting places in Japan, including conventions and museums dedicated to manga and anime.

Japan Times: Manga
www.japantimes.co.jp/tag/manga

The *Japan Times* is a major English-language newspaper in Japan. Its website features recent headlines and stories about manga and related media.

INDEX

IMAGE CREDITS

Cover: © portishead1/iStockphoto
5: © Ned Snowman/Shutterstock Images
7: © enchanted_fairy/Shutterstock Images
9: © InfantryDavid/Shutterstock Images
11: © Reed Means/Shutterstock Images
13: © InfantryDavid/Shutterstock Images
17: © Chiikun Box/Shutterstock Images
19: © Morumotto/Shutterstock Images
21: © Roi and Roi/iStockphoto
23: © TheVisualsYouNeed/Shutterstock Images
25: © Mehmet Bahadir Senemoglu/Shutterstock Images
27: © gary718/Shutterstock Images
29: © poludziber/Shutterstock Images
31: © Gengis90/Shutterstock Images
33: Katsushika Hokusai/H. O. Havemeyer Collection/Met Museum
38: © fluke samed/Shutterstock Images
41: © Will SaeChao/Shutterstock Images
43: © image_vulture/Shutterstock Images
45: © Elena Kharichkina/Shutterstock Images
50: © Mac Odolinski/Shutterstock Images
52: © insta_photos/Shutterstock Images
55: © smolaw/Shutterstock Images
57: © Harsin Isa/SIPA/AP Images
59: © Leafedge/iStockphoto
63: © aijiro/Shutterstock Images
65: © Unique Shutter/Shutterstock Images
67: © Morumotto/Shutterstock Images
70: © Tofudevil/Shutterstock Images
73: © David Tonelson/Shutterstock Images

ABOUT THE AUTHOR

Christine Ha is an artist and writer from Minnesota. She has been a fan of anime and manga from a young age.